CONT

CWA0531616

SOMETHING IS *THERE*

A POEM TO SHARE

Written by Lilian Moore
Illustrated by Philip Webb

Something is there,
there on the stair.
Coming
down,
coming
down,
stepping with care.

Coming
down,
coming
down,
slinkety-sly.
Something is coming
and wants to get by.

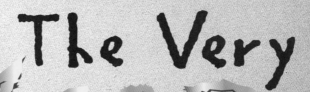

The Very SCARY MONSTER

WRITTEN BY JOY COWLEY
ILLUSTRATED BY MARTIN BAILEY

4

By the lighthouse
was a beach.
By the beach was a town.
By the town was a farm.
By the farm was a hill.

And on top of that hill
lived a very **SCARY** monster.

The very **SCARY** monster
could see the lighthouse.
He didn't like the light
that went wink, wink, wink
all through the night.

"I'll turn it off," he said.

So the very **SCARY** monster
flew down the hill
and across the farm, saying,
"I'm a very **SCARY** monster.
I'm a very **SCARY** monster."

An owl got so scared
that it fell out of its tree.

The cows got so scared
that they ran off
with their tails
in the air.

The very **SCARY** monster
flew through the town
and along the beach, saying,
"I'm a very **SCARY** monster.
I'm a very **SCARY** monster."

A truck driver
got so scared that
he ran over a rubbish bin.

The seagulls
got so scared that
they flew away, screeching.

13

The very **SCARY** monster
flew to the lighthouse.
Wink, wink, wink
went the light.

"Here I come,"
said the monster,
with a monster laugh.
"Here I come
to turn off the light."

The little girl who
lived in the lighthouse
heard the monster coming,
but she was not scared.

She waited behind the door.

The very **SCARY** monster
opened the door
and went in.

"BOO!"
yelled the little girl.

The very **SCARY** monster
got so scared
that he fell backwards
down the stairs.

BUMP!

BUMP!

BUMP!

The very **SCARY** monster
ran away
as fast as he could
along the beach,
through the town,
across the farm,
and up the hill.

The little girl got
back into bed.
And, all through
the night, the light
went wink, wink, wink.

Monster

WRITTEN BY JOY COWLEY
ILLUSTRATED BY PHILIP WEBB

Monster was sick.
She went to the doctor.

"What is your name?"
asked the doctor.
"What work do
you do?"

"My name is Monster,"
said Monster,
"and I do mischief."

"What sort of mischief?"
asked the doctor.

"All sorts," said Monster.

"I pop balloons...

I pick the icing off cakes...

I squeeze the toothpaste
out of tubes...

and I scare the postie!"

"Ah!" said the doctor.
"No wonder you are sick.
You are worn out
with mischief.
You'll have to stop it
at once."

"But I've done mischief
all my life," said Monster.
"I can't give it up now."

"You'll have to try,"
said the doctor.

So Monster tried to give up doing mischief.

She didn't pop balloons.

She didn't pick the icing off cakes.

She didn't squeeze the toothpaste out of tubes.

Now she felt very well!

"The doctor was right,"
said Monster.
"No more mischief
from now on."

But, every now and then,
Monster would forget...

33

and she would
scare the postie!

THE HORRIBLE THING WITH HAIRY FEET

Written by Joy Cowley
Illustrated by Martin Bailey

36

Over the river,
there is a farm, and...

on that farm,
there is a field of thistles.

In that field of thistles,
there is a tin shed, and...

in that tin shed,
there is a rickety floor.

In that rickety floor,
there is a dark hole, and...

in that dark hole,
there is...

40

THE HORRIBLE THING
WITH HAIRY FEET!

One day, a girl
named Lucy...

went over the river
to the farm,

42

across the farm
to the field of thistles,

and through the field
of thistles to the tin shed.

43

She went
into the tin shed and
across the rickety floor.
And she stopped beside
the dark hole.

"Yoo hoo!" called Lucy.
"Who lives here?"
Out jumped...

THE HORRIBLE THING
WITH HAIRY FEET!

"I do!" it said.

"And I'm going to eat you!"

"No, you won't!" said Lucy. She ran across the floor, out of the tin shed,

through the field of thistles,

across the farm,

over the river, and...

she didn't stop running

until she got to town!

The Horrible Thing
with Hairy Feet
laughed and laughed,
because everyone knows
that the Horrible Thing
with Hairy Feet eats only...

chocolate biscuits!